You
and
Your Star Sign

Forum Books Limited
Chobham, Surrey GU24 8RL

"You and Your Star Sign. Scorpio"
Danish edition © Irene Hedlund
and Forlaget Forum A.S.
English edition © Forum Books Limited
English translation by Vivien Andersen
Printed in Spain

ISBN 1-872081-10-X
Novoprint, S. A.
Dep. Legal: B-29896-93

Irene Hedlund

You
and
Your Star Sign

SCORPIO

♏

Forum Books

1

"Are you a Pisces or a Leo?"

"What sign of the Zodiac are you?"

Most people are asked that question at some time or other. And they nearly always know what sign they are.

Sometimes the person asking the question will look at you thoughtfully and say:
"You don't look like one" or "Yes, that fits."

But what does it mean when for instance somebody was born under the sign of Aries? Is it true that Pisceans are different from Leos?

Is it possible to "read" in the stars what is going to happen to you in ten or twenty years time? And why do we use the expression "She was born under a lucky star."?

The people who work with these questions are called ASTROLOGERS. And the science which deals with the significance of the stars is called ASTROLOGY.

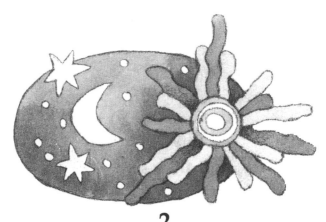

2
What is Astrology?

For thousands of years people have known that the Sun and the Moon influence our lives. And for just as long they have also believed that there is a link between the position of the stars and the planets at the moment of a person's birth and their future chances and destiny.

Even people who don't believe in astrology will admit that their mood differs when there is a full Moon or a new Moon.

Many people believe that astrology tells us what is going to happen in the future, but it isn't as simple as that. Astrology reveals what characteristics you are endowed with. But of course you have the freedom to make what you will of these characteristics, for better or for worse. You can't simply lean back and put the blame on the stars or fate for whatever happens to you in your life.

3
Why be interested in Astrology?

At the moment of your birth you are exposed to influences from the Sun, the Moon, the planets and the stars. These influences determine whether for example you are likely to be hard-working or lazy, untidy or methodical, hot-headed or friendly.

No two people are exposed to the same influences. Even though they may be born at the same time, the planets will be in different positions, depending on where they were born; in London or Madrid perhaps, in Melbourne or New York.

If you want to find out which characteristics you possess, then you can have a NATAL HOROSCOPE cast. This will tell you about your strong and weak characteristics. And then it is up to you whether you want to concentrate on developing your strengths or whether you want to do something about your weaknesses.

So astrology can provide you with a better understanding of your personality. And it can also offer some good advice on how you can develop and fulfil yourself.

4
Your Sun Sign

Long ago, people used to believe that the Sun revolved around the Earth. The huge circular path it completed every year was divided into twelve sections, and each section was given an "animal" name corresponding to the constellations along the Sun's path in the sky, also called the Zodiac. Just look at the table below.

Star	Sign	Period of your birth
♈	Aries	21 March - 20 April
♉	Taurus	21 April - 20 May
♊	Gemini	21 May - 21 June
♋	Cancer	22 June - 22 July
♌	Leo	23 July - 22 August
♍	Virgo	23 August - 23 September
♎	Libra	24 September - 22 October
♏	Scorpio	23 October - 22 November
♐	Sagittarius	23 November - 21 December
♑	Capricorn	22 December - 20 January
♒	Aquarius	21 January - 19 February
♓	Pisces	20 February - 20 March

5
The Four Elements

The twelve signs which are listed in section 4 are divided into four groups called the four 'elements'. Signs belonging to the same element have similar traits.

The four elements are: Fire, Earth, Air and Water. The table below shows you which element your Sun sign belongs to:

Fire : Aries, Leo, Sagittarius
Earth : Taurus, Virgo, Capricorn
Air : Gemini, Libra, Aquarius
Water : Cancer, Scorpio, Pisces

The Fire Element

Fire is the element which makes up the Sun, and the Sun is the source of all life on Earth. So people whose Sun sign is also a Fire sign are full of drive and imagination. They have lively temperaments and always expect a lot of action.

The Earth Element

People whose Sun sign is an Earth sign are very down-to-earth! They don't make any giddy plans or have crazy ideas. They prefer doing something concrete, and are good at making things work.

The Air Element

People whose Sun sign is an Air sign are contemplative, and inquisitive. They love talking, discussing and making plans. The fact that many of their plans are so full of hot air that they are impossible to carry out is quite another matter.

The Water Element

If your sign is a Water sign, you are probably sensitive,   considerate, shy and a day-dreamed. You are romantic and able to sense and understand what others feel. And lots of Water signs are highly creative.

Which other Sun signs do you get on with?

If you want to know who you are likely to get on well with and what sort of people you can make friends with easily, it might be

useful to find out which Sun sign they are born under or what element they belong to.

If you share the same Sun sign, you are likely to have common interests. You will also have roughly the same temperaments, and that can be an advantage, unless of course, you are both equally stubborn and only want to follow your own ideas.

On the other hand it is not nearly as common for couples to share the same Sun sign. It looks as though people are often attracted to their opposites when choosing a girlfriend or boyfriend.

If you belong to the same element you will usually get on well. That does not mean that you won't find friends amongst those who belong to the other elements, though you might get on better with some than with others.

6

The Ascendant

I'm sure you've often met people who behaved in a definite way the first time you met them. They may have been either very confident or very insecure. But then when you got to know them better, they turned out to be completely different.

We all have a side of ourselves which we show in public. We can call this a facade. And this facade can be very different to the person hiding behind it. This has something to do with the **Ascendant.**

What is the Ascendant?

Imagine that at the very moment of your birth you had looked towards the East. The line that your eye would have followed is called the Ascendant. It would have pointed towards a particular sign of the Zodiac.

As the earth revolves on its axis once every 24 hours, the Ascendant will travel through all 12 signs of the Zodiac every 24 hours. So every day each sign appears in the Ascendant for just two hours.

For instance, if you are an Arian with Cancer in the Ascendant, it means that you may act like a Cancer person on the surface, even though deep down you are an Arian. And since Cancerians are soft and sensitive, whilst Arians are impetuous and hot-headed, it can be difficult for others to guess your Sun sign. So it wouldn't be possible to make an accurate guess before one knew you really well.

How can you find out which sign of the Zodiac is in your Ascendant?

First of all, you have to know the exact time of day when you were born. Ask your parents - they are bound to remember.

Maybe you know somebody who is interested in Astrology. Nowadays most astrologers use computers, and the astrology programmes are designed to work out the sign in the Ascendant in a matter of seconds.

You can also work it out yourself, but this method is not quite as accurate as a computer. To work it out you will need to use the two discs on the next page. The first disc consists of two rings; the outer one shows the twelve signs of the Zodiac, the inner one the names of the months.

The other disc shows the 24 hours of the day.

Make a photocopy of the page. Glue the paper onto a piece of cardboard and cut out the two discs. You will see that the small disc just fits inside the large one.

Put a pin through the middle of the small disc so that it can rotate inside the larger one.

Let us imagine that your birthday is on the 15th of April and that you were born at 11 o'clock in the morning. Now move the inner disc so that the arrow points to the middle of the month of April.

Next, find the hour of your birth. In our example it was 11 a.m. In the outer ring you will find the sign Leo opposite 11 a.m. That is the sign you have in the Ascendant.

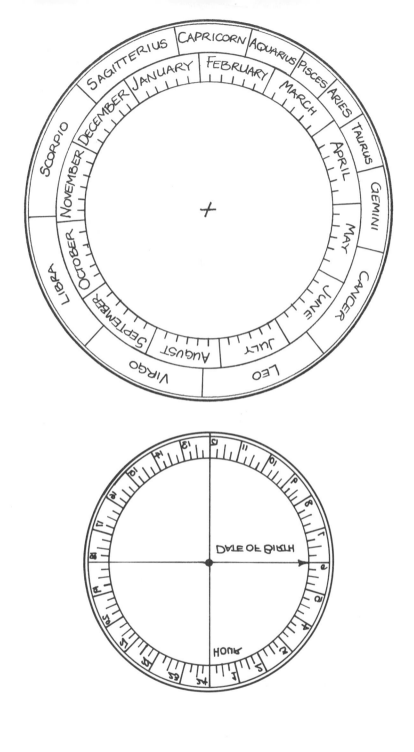

Now you know both your Sun sign and the sign you have in the Ascendant. Or in other words, you can now work out how you appear to other people, and what are your true characteristics.

7
Does everyone born under the same sign of the Zodiac have the same characteristics?

Of course not everyone born under the same sign will have the same character. Everyone is also influenced by the Moon and the planets, which will have been in different positions at the time of their birth.

But as the Sun sign is the strongest of all the signs, people who are born under the same sign will share many of the same character traits.

For instance, if you are an Arian, and you have read what Arians are like, you may sometimes have thought to yourself, "I'm not like that at all!" You may have read that Arians have leadership qualities, and that therefore they always get their own way. But you may feel quite the opposite, and that it is nearly always you who gives in to others.

This may be because many of your friends are also Arians. And the influences of the planets on them make them even "stronger" than you. Or perhaps some of the planets' other influences tend to have a contrary effect on the way you behave.

Perhaps you don't always act according to your nature, but rather according to how you think other people would like you to be.

It could also be that someone has been told, that according to his or her horoscope, he or she is a spendthrift. That person then may make a conscious effort to be more economical. So in this way he or she uses astrology to change for the better.

Finally however, you must realise, that however many books you read about astrology, only a natal horoscope cast by an astrologer can provide you with an accurate picture of your own personal horoscope.

8
Signs of the Zodiac and Gemstones

Some people believe that there is a connection between the signs of the Zodiac and gemstones. So if you want to have a lucky stone, it's a good idea to choose one which fits your Star sign. Some people even believe that wearing the right stone can help protect them against all sorts of diseases.

These are the gemstones and colours which belong to your star sign:

Aries
Quartz, Agate, Diamonds and Jasper.
Colour: red.

Taurus
Rose Quartz and Sapphire.
Colours: green, pink and brownish hues.

Gemini
Light Agate, Sapphire.
Golden colours.

Cancer
Amethyst, Emerald and Moonstone.
Colours: orange, light grey or silver.

Leo

Aquamarine, Amber and Topaz.
Colours: yellow, orange and gold.

Virgo

Agate, Diamond.
Colours: green, brown and dark hues.

Libra

Opal and Turquoise.
Colours: pink, green, light colours.

Scorpio

Garnet, Emerald and Tiger-eye.
Colours: white, black, gold and silver.

Sagittarius

Lapis Lazuli and Topaz.
Colours: orange, yellow and blue.

Capricorn

Agate, Onyx and Ruby.
Colours: green and black.

Aquarius

Amethyst, Garnet and Ruby.
Colours: bluish-green hues.

Pisces

Amethyst, Amazonite.
Colours: mauve and pink.

Scorpio
23rd October - 22nd November

How can you tell a Scorpio?

If you tell a group of people that you are good at detecting which Star sign they belong to, there will always be somebody who will try to catch your eye and claim that you definitely won't be able to guess his. Say "Scorpio" and you will probably be right.

There are other ways of telling a Scorpio. Most people do not like losing at games, but if you meet someone who considers any defeat to be a total catastrophe, that person will probably turn out to be a Scorpio. Scorpions hate to lose.

Scorpions also hate false modesty, so if you ask one whether they are good at something or other and they think they are, they will say so straight out. And if you want their opinion about your latest hairstyle or boyfriend, you will get an equally honest answer. Scorpions will not

resort to flattery just to obtain something. That is beneath their dignity.

Some people are too embarrassed to admit that they are Scorpions, because the Scorpion is a creature who attacks his victim and kills it with the poison sitting in its tail. If it finds itself cornered it will even turn its poison onto itself.

But there really is no reason to be ashamed about being a Scorpion. A Scorpion who has had a loving home will develop into a friendly, caring person.

Scorpions are incredibly inquisitive. For instance they want to know what other people are thinking, and they will go on asking until they get an answer. And there is no point in trying to fool a Scorpion, because they will see through any deception straight away.

Scorpio Children

Scorpions have good memories, and will remember your kindnesses as well as your cruelties. Your generosity will be richly rewarded, but you can expect dreadful revenge to be taken if you have been nasty. Just try to make fun of a Scorpion in public and you will find that you will receive a dose of your own medicine - with interest.

Scorpion children love dangerous games, and so they inevitably have accidents. But they are not cowards and they don't howl or scream if they have to have a cut cleaned or a couple of stitches.

Scorpio children love monsters and horror films, and they prefer ghost stories to fairy tales any day.

Scorpions in School

As Scorpions hate to lose, they also try to be amongst the best at school. They have a lot of energy and really make an effort to attain the goals they have set themselves.

Scorpions tend to be extremist. No-one can hate as much as a Scorpion who feels

that he or she has been victimized. And problems may arise in school if the Scorpion gets on the wrong side of teachers or friends. But Scorpions are also willing to go through hell and high water for those they like.

Work and Leisure Activities

Scorpions love secrets, so detective stories or TV thrillers are just their cup of tea.

They do not always aspire to the top jobs at work. But they do like to be in control and so they prefer to pull the strings and direct things the way they want.

Scorpions are also attracted by danger in their choice of jobs. Many of them attempt to realise their childhood dreams and end up as soldiers, policemen or firemen.

But their great interest in other people's emotional lives also leads them to jobs as psychologists, lawyers or social workers.

Good Advice

Scorpio people would do both themselves and others a favour if they learned to control

their tempers. That goes for when they are playing games and think they are about to lose, as well as when they think they have been unfairly treated by others.

Friendship

Scorpions often do not have a lot of friends, because they are very fussy and can easily see through people. On the other hand, once you have been accepted by a Scorpion, he or she will become a very faithful friend.

If you are friends with a Scorpion, do not expect to keep many secrets. For instance, if

you have fallen for the new person in your class, it will not be long before your Scorpio friend has sussed it out. He or she is not only good at guessing other people's feelings, but is also extremely inquisitive.

But do not try to stick your nose too deeply into the Scorpion's private life. Scorpions do not like that at all. For as much as they like to guess your secrets, they want to guard their own.

Love

If you are a boy who has attracted a Scorpio girl, you must be someone really special. Because she will not settle for any old Tom, Dick or Harry. And if you break up, your next girlfriend will have quite a lot to live up to.

For Scorpions are never boring companions. They are very emotional and when they fall in love they do so with such ardour that it can quite take one's breath away.

But there is also a reverse side to their emotions. Scorpions get jealous very quickly, and their anger will erupt like a volcano if they have even the slightest suspicion that you have been flirting with somebody else. And even if you are quite innocent, the suspicion can be so powerful that it will break up your relationship.

Scorpions love to be in control of their lives. They want to run everything themselves, even their love lives. You must expect that your Scorpion sweetheart will want to satisfy his or her own needs first before considering yours. But once committed, he or she will be extra sweet and loving.

Who do you get on well with?

Good friends are often born under the same Sun sign, or at any rate belong to the same element. Scorpio is a Water sign, so this means that Scorpions get on well with other Water signs, Pisces and Cancer.

It is not nearly as common for couples to share the same Sun sign as friends often do. When it comes to choosing a partner, it looks as though many people are attracted by their opposites.

Water and Air

The Air signs, Gemini, Libra and Aquarius, can learn a lot from the Water signs, and vice versa. For example, Scorpions find it hard to grasp that other people are different to them and don't think the way they do. Air sign people are much more understanding. But Water sign people can teach Air sign people to recognise their own emotions.

Water and Air get on well with each other, but just as water can have a suffocating effect on air for you cannot breathe under water, a Scorpion can be so dominating that an Air sign person feels stifled.

On the other hand, the air can whip up great storms and high seas. And this can happen if an Aquarian or a Libran is not sufficiently aware of Scorpion sensitivity, which may provoke a Scorpion tempest.

Of all the Air signs, Scorpions get on best with Geminis.

Water and Earth

Water is necessary for all growth on earth.

This means that people born under an Earth sign usually get on well with Scorpions. Earth sign people are down-to-earth and sensible, and Scorpions are more emotional. So if they do not pressurise each other too much but respect each other's idosyncrasies, they can derive much pleasure from each other.

But just as a plant will wilt and die if it is not watered, a friendship will also flounder if the Scorpion gives free rein to his emotions without showing consideration for his more down-to-earth Taurean friends.

Of all the Earth signs, Scorpions usually get on best with Capricorns or Virgos.

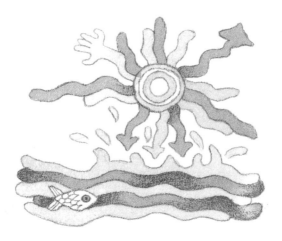

Water and Fire

These two signs are not normally well suited. Water puts out fire. Scorpions just cannot cope with an Arian or a Leo who comes charging in with some half-baked project to be carried out right away.

In return, Fire sign people are irritated by the thoroughness and systematic nature of the Scorpions.

But of course we don't want you to drop all your mates and friends who don't belong to the 'right' sign. For even though you may be very different, it doesn't necessarily mean that you are going to quarrel.

On the contrary, you can grow to understand those who think differently to you. And perhaps they can help you with things you are not so good at.

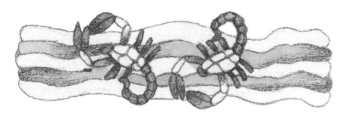

Famous Scorpions

Boris Becker	Tennis player
Georges Bizet	Composer
Richard Burton	Actor
Prince Charles	Prince of Wales
John Cleese	Comedian
Captain James Cook	Explorer
Marie Curie	Physicist
Bob Hoskins	Actor
Mahalia Jackson	Gospel singer
Grace Kelly	Actress
Burt Lancaster	Actor
Claude Monet	Painter
Theodore Roosevelt	US president
Leon Trotsky	Communist leader
Jan Vermeer	Painter